Piano Sight-Reading for Adult Beginners

Fast Learning Techniques

Matteo Malafronte

2022 | All Copyrights Reserved Matteo Malafronte

All rights reserved. No part of this book may be reproduced, scanned, or distributed in any printed or electronic form without permission.

CONTENTS

5	**Curriculum**
6	**Chapter 1**
7	1.1 The fixity points of the sight
9	1.2 The Musical Alphabet
24	1.3 The Musical Alphabet and the staff

pIAnO

SIGHT-READING

FOR ADULT BEGINNERS

Matteo Malafronte

Curriculum

Matteo Malafronte is in close contact with the pedagogical legacy of the legendary Neapolitan pianist Maria Tipo, having been for several years pupil of pianists successors of her tradition: firstly of Maestro Giuseppe Andaloro, winner of the Busoni Prize (President of the Commission: Maria Tipo), then of Maestro Alessandro Marangoni, who perfected with Maria Tipo at Fiesole School of Music, and finally of Maestro Luca De Gregorio, who studied with the great Neapolitan teacher in Switzerland, at the Conservatoire Supérieur de Musique of Geneva. In 2020, at the age of 23, he published the didactic manual "Metodo di Lettura Pianistica" (Trans. "Piano Reading Method". MALAFRONTE, Matteo. Metodo di Lettura Pianistica. Poland: Amazon Fulfillment, 2020), which received wide approval: on November 26 of the same year, "Metodo di Lettura Pianistica" ranks #1 in the Amazon Kindle IT "Music" category, alongside highly authoritative texts. In addition to his collaborations with national bodies and festivals, we highlight the recording activities (CENTORIO, Marco Antonio; HEREDIA, Pietro. Mottetti, Inni e Antifone. London: Elegia, 2019) and the managing of important social network channels, counting more than hundreds of thousands of visits.

Chapter

1

1.1
The fixity points of the sight

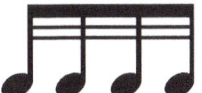

If we wanted to determine the speed at which a pianist reads written music, we would need to know how fast he or she could understand it. In a neophyte, however, the understanding of musical language is not often as immediate as it is for words. We have been taught as children to read and write letters, then to combine them into syllables, then to build words, sentences… Let's go back in our memories for a second to remember how many hours we spent at school just to learn how to write a simple sentence. The art of combining letters, syllables and words into meanings has required a lot of time for each of us to be mastered, and if we are now here reading fast as lightning hundreds and hundreds of characters in just a few seconds, it is because we became expert at understanding them. In reading a musical score, the same thing happens: it is not enough to mechanically learn by heart or to perfectly know all the elements of musical theory, but rather, we must understand the role of those elements within the context in which they are placed. This does not mean that we should sit comfortably and not practice anything we read in this handbook, but instead we must give the right space to both method and application. Let's take repetition as an example: any musician, at some point in his career, has faced the situation of having to repeat a passage over and over in order to read it better, play it better, understand it better. Now imagine repeating a hundred times a whole composition or a passage in a way that was wrong from the very beginning! We would get more harm than good. So the time alone is not enough if there is no method. Vice versa: imagine spending hours and hours reading this book without putting into practice anything written in it! Again, we would get more harm than good. Balancing method and application is not easy at all: since both are essential but cannot be cultivated at the same time, it is necessary to set priorities in order to understand when to cultivate one or the other.

With this premise, it is easier to understand why we start our journey from the following consideration: in addition to being able to understand music, you must also know how to outline the elements that compose it, and must be able, while reading, to keep your eye steady for the shortest time possible. But this aspect is not decisive since it always depends on a precise awareness in the brain, that is, on comprehension. Imagine that we have to quickly outline something whose shape is completely unknown! That's how it is: sometimes academies teach that "it is essential to accustom the eye to always look ahead of what you are reading"; or that "the eye should never stop or turn back when reading"… These teachings must not be misunderstood: never forget that it is always the brain that controls the eye, and if the brain is asked to stop or turn back, it is not by mechanically accustoming the eye to look only "ahead" that one acquires confidence in reading; especially since, at the beginning, "ahead" for a neophyte can simply mean a little more to the right, or at the end, or on the next page… Instructions whose generality hides from us the real meaning of the words of the teacher: if presented in this way, they only accustom the body to prevail over the mind.

1.2
The Musical Alphabet

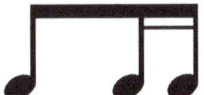

The very fact that we are reading these lines proves that we are already able to efficiently practice the names of the notes. These, in fact, are nothing more than words.

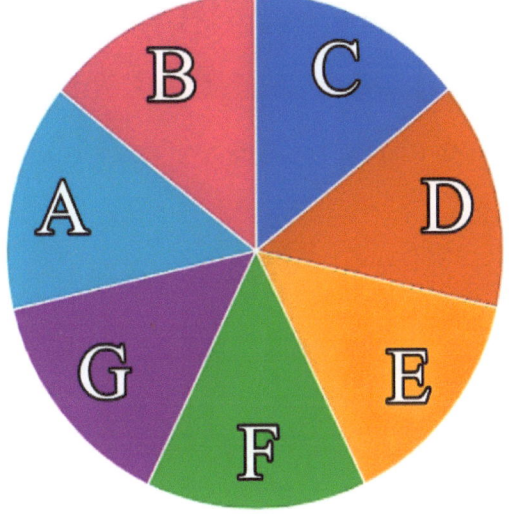

Figure 1

No sounds and no rhythms, just words. The seven names constitute the Musical Alphabet, which we must imagine just as it is pictured above: in a circular shape. In popular culture, the notes are mainly represented by sounds or specific graphic signs and only rarely by names, yet these play a key role in musical reading. For this reason, we must start by separating the components of music from their most popular symbols, which are quite often simplifications. In order to do this, the first step is understanding the elements that constitute the notes. Some of them will be the pillars of your reading ability, but you won't know which ones until you have mastered them all. For some people, it is enough to be familiar with the sounds to be able to properly read a sheet of music; for others, it is first of all necessary to know the names, and so on. Let's start the research from the Musical Alphabet: as we can see from the figure above, the Musical Alphabet does not have a starting point or a direction; for the moment it's up to us to decide the point - or points - from which we begin and end the reading. This characteristic is what makes it very different from the simple sequence of names we have known since childhood, A – B – C – D – E – F – G. In fact, this sequence, which many people know even if they have never taken a sheet of music in their hands, has a precise starting point and a precise ending point. But there is only one case in which we read the Musical Alphabet as A – B – C – D – E – F – G, that is, when we start from A and read clockwise to G. Think for a moment how many other possibilities for pronouncing notes' names we may have ignored.

Exercise 1[1]

While looking at the figure, slowly pronounce each name of the Musical Alphabet three times, each time following the name on its right. For example, starting from A, you would say *A – B – A – B – A – B*; starting from C you would say *C – D – C – D – C – D*. When you know by heart which letter comes next, begin to quickly perform entire rounds of the Musical Alphabet as in the example below:

A-B-*B*-C-*C*-D-*D*-E-*E*-F-*F*-G-*G*-A…

B-C-*C*-D-*D*-E-*E*-F-*F*-G-*G*-A-*A*-B…

---

[1] In the exercises, pay attention to the names in **bold**: it's on those notes that you need to put emphasis when you practice.

From now on, even though it will not always be specified, never practice an exercise without first completing the previous one: proceed only when you become confident at both low and high speed. For example, to complete this first exercise you should be able to pronounce each group smoothly and by heart: first within two seconds, then within half a second. The Musical Alphabet is only the first of several components that constitute the notes: only after learning to recognize them all we will start to connect them together. A note is a complex connection of elements, which is why in most cases it is counterproductive to learn to read music directly by playing a music score. Many children who start playing piano abandon it as they get older: in some cases, the difficulties in reading have been increased by the excessive levity with which they have been accustomed to approach the instrument, preventing the child from understanding the mistakes it makes. This is also true for those who did not start playing as children: we wish to read music, but we are often introduced to this art by someone who only puts four notes directly in front of us as if it was just a trivial exercise of repetition. But let's think about it: even if there were only four notes, these are composed not only of names but also of sounds. With a simple multiplication, we are now in front of eight different elements! And the number would significantly increase if we knew all the components of musical reading that we have not yet been taught to recognize. Imagine a great footballer, a forward with legendary ball control, with physical power and incomparable quickness in running, capable of dribbling opponents in the most brilliant ways: he is certainly a phenomenon, we would say... But we would not say the same if we discovered that this footballer does not know where the goal is. With this last clarification, if earlier in our minds were running images of the greatest footballer in history, now we are probably thinking "what a waste, he would need so little to be an unforgettable athlete!". None would ever want to be like this football player who, of all the characteristics he needs to be a champion, neglects only one, the one that affects the rest of them. This is why it is counterproductive to learn directly by reading a music score without knowing the elements of the reading process. In most cases we are unable to read notes fluently for this very reason and not because, as some bad teachers would have us believe, we did not start as children or because we lack the talent.

Exercise 2

Choose a name from the figure above. Pronounce the type of Musical Alphabet that is created by reading clockwise back to the starting point. For example, if we choose D we will get: ***D-E-F-G-A-B-C-D***. Try to repeat this exercise starting with each of the note names, first looking at the figure, then by heart.

Some of us have probably already heard the terms *Major Scale* and *Minor Scale*, even if only as children, in cartoons, at school, on the internet. Let's ignore these terms completely for the moment, as they could cause great confusion in the much simpler concept of the Musical Alphabet: a scale that you can't even play because it's just a simple set of words.

Exercise 3

Repeat exercise 1 and exercise 2 on the Musical Alphabet first skipping one note, then two, three, four, five, six and seven notes. If we skip one note, the first part of exercise 1 will be:

C-E, E-G, G-B...

While for exercise 2 we will have:

D-F, F-A, A-C...

In the future, when reading music, it will be the written music to give us all these instructions and we will no longer be the ones making decisions. The next exercise will prepare you to perform more complex tasks.

Exercise 4

Repeat all the previous exercises on the Musical Alphabet following the counterclockwise direction of the figure. For example, Exercise 1 will no longer be *A-B, B-C, C-D*, but *A-G, G-F, F-E* and so on; exercise 2 will no longer be *A-B-C-D-E-F-G-A*, but *A-G-F-E-D-C-B-A*.

Exercise 5

Perfect the previous exercises, clockwise and counterclockwise, completing a double turn of the Musical Alphabet where possible. For example, exercise number two clockwise will become:

F-G-A-B-C-D-E-F-G-A-B-C-D-E-F

The first given example in exercise 3 will be:

C-E-E-G-G-B-B-D-D-F-F-A-A-C-C-E-E-G-G-B-B-D-D-F-F-A-A-C-C-E.

In the following subchapter, we will see that the exercises on the pronunciation of the *names of notes* are absolutely necessary in order to learn to read music fluently: for this reason, they are recommended by the most authoritative textbooks of the past. On the contrary, very few of today's manuals focus for so long on this aspect, which was considered by the most authoritative teachers of the past as an essential didactic premise. In fact, the seven *names of the notes* that compose the *Musical Alphabet* are a prerequisite for the simplest compositions, such as those for beginners, but also for the most complex ones, such as *Rachmaninov's Third Concerto for Piano and Orchestra*. In other words, there are no more than seven note names in the compositions[2] that we will be studying from this point forward. Each one will always combine with one of the following adjectives:

| Double sharp |
| Sharp |
| Natural |
| Flat |
| Double flat |

For the moment, let's just say that these adjectives are called *accidentals* or *signs of alteration*[3]. Here are some examples:

Name of the notes	Adjective
C	Sharp
F	Natural
B	Flat

---

2   The *compositions* of the *common practice period*, i.e. that historical period which, according to Walter Piston, goes from the 18th to the 20th Century. This time span represents an important starting point for the music we listen to today: during these few centuries, almost every elementary piano study has been written, still adopted by most of the Masters for the first exercises of their students - inside and outside the academic environment of the Conservatories.

3   [In this manual, the first term refers to graphic signs, while the second refers to the acoustic effect produced on sound by such signs. Therefore, the two terms will be employed as synonyms only in specific contexts]

At this early stage of the work, we need to imagine such adjectives only as words, without wondering too much about their musical meaning. When a person is telling us their name, we rarely think about the thousands of linguistic implications of it. Similarly, in my experience, I have found that expecting to immediately know both the name and the musical meaning of these simple adjectives can be highly counterproductive.

Exercise 6

Memorize the adjectives of the note names written in the table above.

It goes without saying that many contemporary manuals, even among the Best Sellers, at this point would have already shown an illustration of the piano keyboard, introducing in a single mess all the elements we have dealt with so far, including note names, adjectives of note names, names of the author's cats and dogs... This would have completely prevented us from isolating the elements that we consciously and unconsciously apply to read music. For the moment, we have become fluent in the pronunciation of note names - clockwise and counterclockwise; we have memorized the adjectives that go together to the names of notes; and we have laid some of the necessary foundations for at least three fundamental associations:

1) Association of the seven names of the notes, called Musical Alphabet, with their position on the *staff*[4].

2) Association of the seven names of notes with their position on the white keys of the piano

3) Relation between the first two phases of association.

This is not an exhaustive list. There are different kinds of associations that you will meet during your learning journey. We will address the first one in the next subchapter, while the others are not covered by this volume, but you will find them in the next ones.

---

4   Translator's note: the *staff* is also called *Pentagram* or *stave*.

1.3
The Musical Alphabet and the staff

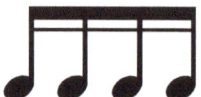

The *staff* [fig. 2] is used in the same way as the Musical Alphabet: the number of lines and spaces we read on the staff, upwards or downwards, would be the same number of letters read on the Musical Alphabet.

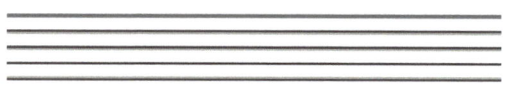

Figure 2

Even if it is commonly considered a sort of container in which notes are written, the staff is instead an integral part of them in the process of musical reading. The staff defines how many names we have to read, in which position of the Musical Alphabet we are, and whether we have to read it clockwise or counterclockwise. But it could not do this all by itself: unlike the Musical Alphabet, where the names are clearly indicated and they clearly distinguish all the seven slices of the chart, on the staff we have anonymous lines and spaces. Looking at the figure above [fig. 2] we could interpret any line or space as any name of note from which we could start reading, but this would mean proceeding randomly. For this reason, the staff cannot be separated in the reading process from the *Clef*. To use a metaphor, clef and staff are the cinematographic set of the Musical Alphabet: since the latter has the potential to endlessly repeat itself in circles, they frame, together, a small portion of it so that we can read within well-defined margins.

Continuing with the metaphor, this framing can be expanded to cover many repetitions of the Musical Alphabet: this is the case of the *Grand staff*, which includes the *treble clef* and the *bass clef* [Fig. 3].

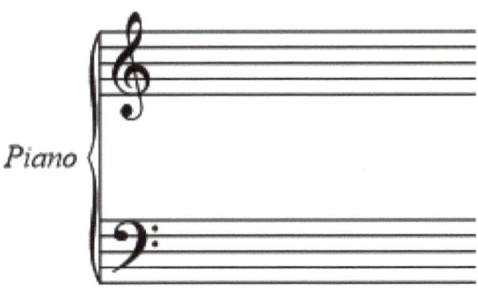

Figure 3

The bass clef tells us that the fourth line starting from the bottom is an *F*. Starting there, and going upward, we encounter the C on the first *ledger line* [Fig. 4]:

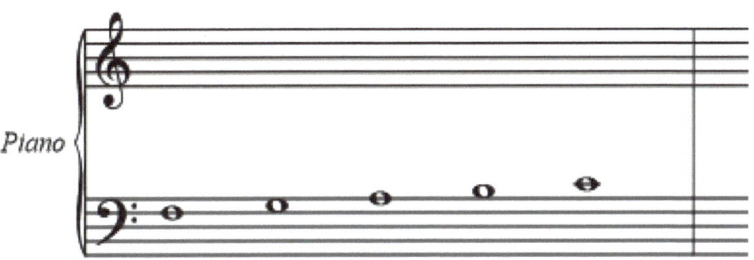

Figure 4

Vice versa, starting from the *G* line indicated by the *treble clef*, we get the same result [Fig. 5]:

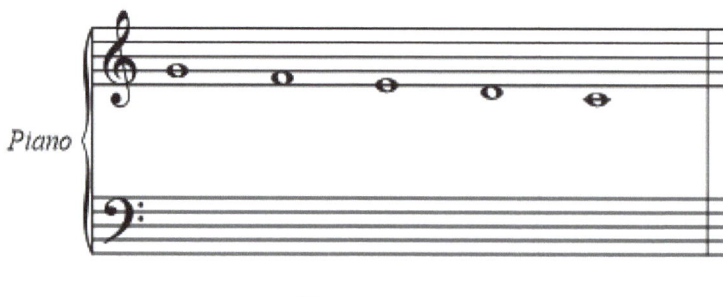

Figure 5

From fig. 5 we can correctly suppose that we will meet a note name at least twice: once starting from the *bass clef* and once starting from the *treble clef*. The two staves are then not to be considered as separate entities but as having a common point. This is evidenced by the fact that reading from that point on, either upward or downward, the names of all lines and all spaces are read the same way in both *clefs*. This means that, since an unlimited number of *ledger lines* can be used, every note placed in the *bass clef* can be written in the *treble clef* and vice versa. Luckily, in the piano exercises for beginners we rarely go beyond three ledger lines in the two clefs. If overstepping the three ledger lines is rare at first, we should know instead that within three upward or downward ledger lines we find the same note no more than three times. For example, G, remaining within the range of three upward or downward ledger lines, is found in these three cases [Fig. 6]:

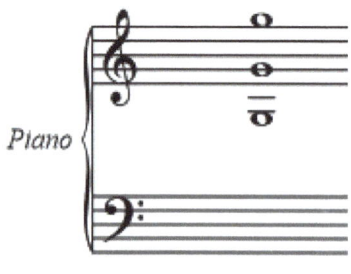

Figure 6

These are the three *G*s that can be met in the *treble clef*, staying within the range of the three *ledger lines*.

Here is another example with the name *B* [fig. 7]:

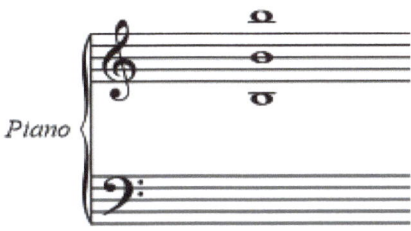

Figure 7

In this regard, let's observe the diagram below, which shows all the three positions of the note names within the three ledger lines:

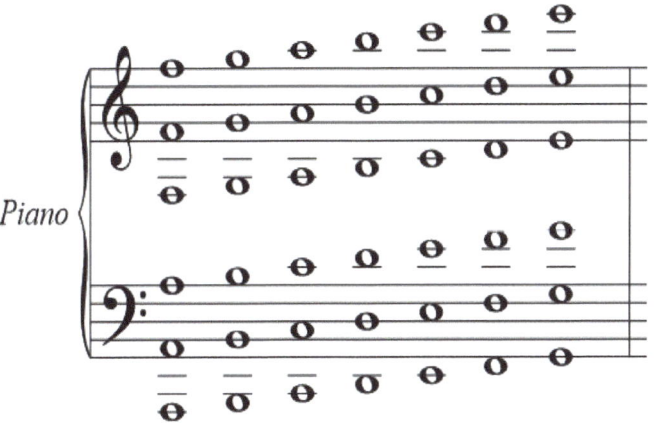

Figure 8

After counting no less than forty-two different positions in the diagram above [fig. 8], it is easy to understand why many of us may require weeks, months, or even years to learn to associate note names to the staff. The risk is that this difficulty may keep being present at a more advanced level of studies, where the limit of ledger lines extends well beyond the number of three. It is not uncommon for this to happen to an adult learner, as he or she is often a victim of the rush to start a piece of repertoire, feeling not to have any more time to dwell on the rudiments of music. The good news is that as far as note names are concerned, there is no real time frame for learning the forty-two basic positions: it depends on which method you adopt for memorization work. In the following exercise we will practice a relatively quick practice method, which I personally devised. If we want to draw an average from my teaching experience, this technique allows the memorization of the forty-two basic nominal positions [fig. 8] in a period of time ranging from three to six days.

Suppose that you want to memorize the respective three positions of B and G in the treble clef [fig. 6 and 7]. In order to do this, all you have to do is create in your mind a painting full of images, sensations, and sounds. It will be quite fun and rewarding. Here's how you should proceed:

Exercise 7

1) Look carefully at the picture below.

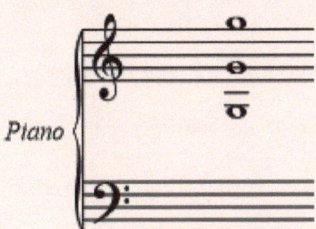

You can associate the three G positions to a concept that starts with the same letter and that will help the memorization of the position of the notes on the staff. In this case, you can associate it with the word "Glow" and start picturing the dot on the second line as a *glowing* setting sun.

2) Create a painting in your mind starting from the word "Glow" and correlate it to the three dots on the score: you can imagine the bottom dot as a reflection of the sun on the sea. Can you see the two ledger lines as a reflection of two glowing rays of sunshine on the ripples at the surface of the sea? They must be exactly two. Imagine. What about the top dot? It could be one of those glowing lens flares that cameras, when framing the sun, capture in a photo.

3) Expand your image, make it richer and add more and more details: experience it intensely. This is the only way for the elements of your imagination to recall each other. For example, the staff could be a set of five clouds. The G on the second line of the staff would therefore be a sun immersed in the clouds, which emerges piercing the second of them from below. Draw what you imagine with a pencil: find every way to make this picture as vivid as possible. Are you imagining? There is a glowing sun in the center, immersed in the second of five clouds: above, a glowing lens flare in the blue sky, outside the clouds; below, on the surface of the sea, two warm glares are reflected on the ripples… Next to you, below the two ripples, the round, glowing shape of the sun is clearly reflected on the water. Why not go for a swim? Why not catch those two waves that are blinding you with their white glares? Why not splash around in the water? Keep imagining. Taste the sea, feel the warmth of the sun. Live this image intensely, also by bringing a loved one with you in your imagination.

4) If you can't picture anything with the pattern that the positions of the notes are forming, then rotate the score, observe it from every angle. Take for example the note name *B*: let's pretend that you observe its three positions and can't immediately find their ideogrammatic meaning [fig. 10]. You'll rotate it ninety degrees, and get this:

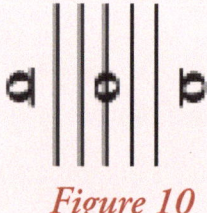

Figure 10

The ideogram in Fig. 10 can be seen as a face of which the central dot is the nose and the two additional cuts are the sides of a face with large protruding ears [Fig. 11].

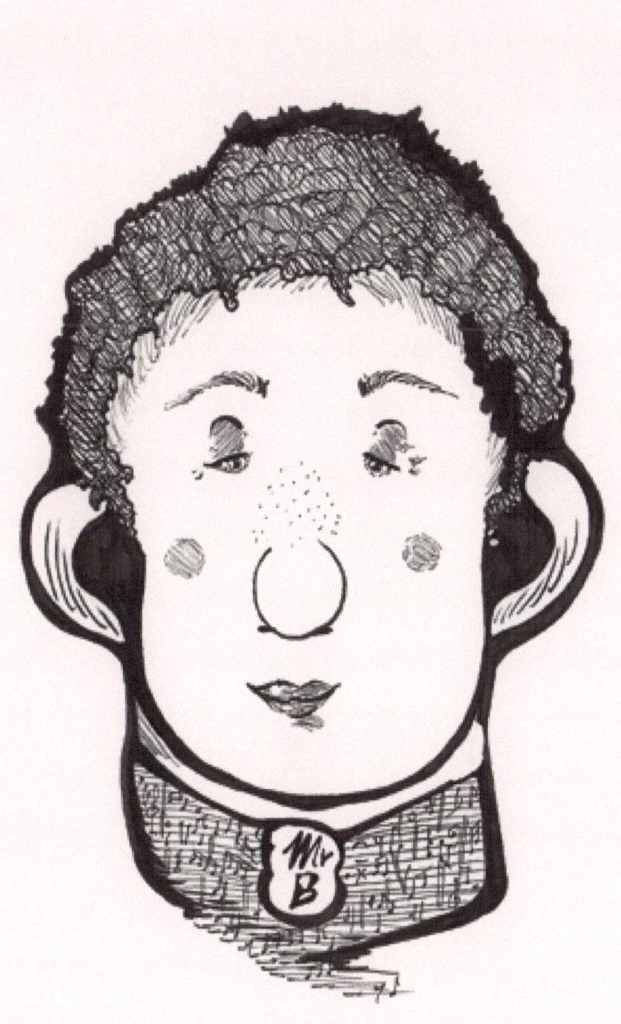

Figure 11

5) Imagine these *big* ears swaying up and down as this *big* face says "Boo", with a nose so *big* it sways until it hits his chin and forehead with every nod. Laugh at your scenario, or cry; in other words: get emotional by picturing your creation. Associate it in your imagination with someone you know, never forgetting how *big* his ears, nose and face are.

6) One last note: for rhythmic reasons, you should know that these dots with which we have represented the position of the note names on the staff can be either empty or full. The note B could therefore be indicated with an empty or full dot. Here is an example for both cases:

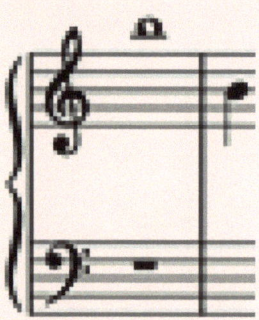

Figure 12

Therefore, try not to base your associations on the emptiness of the dot or on the presence or absence of a line inside it. For example, it is easy to imagine these dots as empty rings: however, for the reasons explained [fig. 12] this is not a particularly effective image because it is not applicable in every case of reading.

Exercise 8

After actively imagining what was described in the previous exercise, practice below to identify the images you associated with the various positions of the note names on the staff. Be careful: you won't have to identify the names, only the images. For example, if you read this:

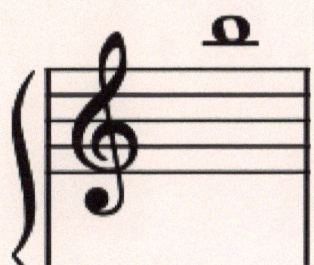

You won't have to say: it's a B. Instead, you will have to say: it is the ear of the face that says "Boo"

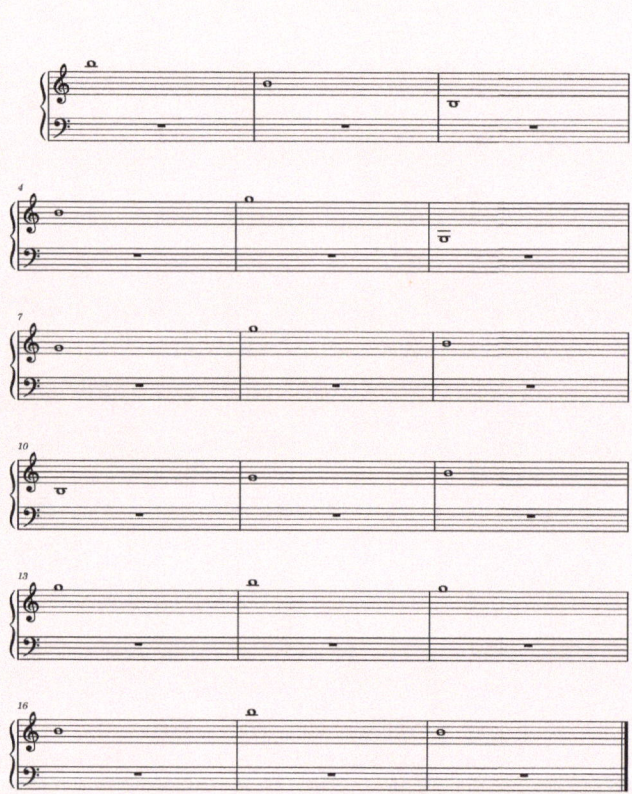

Solutions: ear, nose, ear, nose, lens flare, glares, sun, lens flare, nose, ear, sun, nose, lens flare, ear, lens flare, nose, ear, nose.

Perform the exercise also in the opposite direction, starting from different points of the exercise. Once you feel ready, start reading directly the names of the notes, always remembering to evoke the associated image in your mind. It will take some time and practice before you will stop thinking about the associated image. But the process will be automatic: at a certain point of your practice you will realize that you no longer need two steps.

When you feel prepared and have perfected all the exercises, proceed to the next volume, where we will cover the other associations previously mentioned.

More Content On

www.matteomalafronte.com

www.ingramcontent.com/pod-product-compliance
Lightning Source LLC
Chambersburg PA
CBHW041934240526
45473CB00034B/1646